Bath and West of England Society

Rules, Orders, and Premiums, of the Bath Society

For the Encouragement of Agriculture, Arts, Manufacture, and Commerce...

Bath and West of England Society

Rules, Orders, and Premiums, of the Bath Society
For the Encouragement of Agriculture, Arts, Manufacture, and Commerce...

ISBN/EAN: 9783744677349

Printed in Europe, USA, Canada, Australia, Japan

Cover: Foto ©Suzi / pixelio.de

More available books at **www.hansebooks.com**

RULES, ORDERS,

AND

PREMIUMS,

OF THE

BATH SOCIETY,

FOR THE ENCOURAGEMENT OF

AGRICULTURE, ARTS, MANUFACTURES, And COMMERCE,

IN THE COUNTIES OF

SOMERSET, WILTS, GLOCESTER, AND DORSET,

AND THE

CITY AND COUNTY OF *BRISTOL:*

WITH

A LIST OF THE MEMBERS OF THE SOCIETY,

AND OF THE PREMIUMS GRANTED IN 1789.

BATH, PRINTED BY R. CRUTTWELL,

BY ORDER OF THE SOCIETY.

M DCC XC.

OFFICERS OF THE SOCIETY.

PRESIDENT,

The Right Hon. the Earl of AILESBURY.

VICE-PRESIDENTS,

Sir William Jones, Bart.
Sir John Riggs Miller, Bart.
Sir John Smith, Bart.
Sir John Guiſe, Bart.
Sir John Durbin
Matthew Brickdale, Eſq;
John Billingſley, Eſq;
W. Falconer, M. D, F. R. S.
Samuel Cam, Eſq;
A. Fothergill, M. D. F. R. S.
Henry Hippiſley Coxe, Eſq;
Rev. M. Stafford Smith
Benjamin Colborne, Eſq;
Abel Moyſey, Eſq;
Charles Phillot, Eſq;
James Stephens, Eſq;
Luck Anningſon, Eſq;
James Sutton, Eſq;
Iſaac Webb Horlock, Eſq;
W. Watſon, eſq; F. R. S.
Joſeph Harford, Eſq;
Daniel Lyſons, M. D.
John Anſtie, Eſq;
William Clavill, Eſq.

SECRETARY,

WIILLIAM MATTHEWS.

COMMITTEE

COMMITTEE

On AGRICULTURE and PLANTING.

Baron Dimſdale
Sir John Riggs Miller, Bart.
Benjamin Colborne, Eſq;
W. Falconer, M. D. F. R. S.
A. Fothergill, M. D. F. R. S.
William Watſon, Eſq;
James Stephens, Eſq;
W. Aldridge Ballard, Eſq;
John Billingſley, Eſq;
Gaisford Gibbs, Eſq;
Joſeph Harford, Eſq;
Daniel Lyſons, M. D.
William Whitaker, Eſq;
Rev. Thomas Broughton
Rev Mr. Brookes
James Sutton, Eſq;
Luck Anningſon, Eſq;
Samuel Cam, Eſq;
Thomas Davis, Eſq;
Mr. Parſons, *Blagdon*
Mr. James Smith
Mr. Thomas Robins
Mr. William Peacey
Mr. Henry Vagg
Mr. George Barnes
Mr. Joſiah Hazard
Mr. William Clark
William Croſely, Eſq;
Michael Hicks, Eſq;
William Dyke, Eſq.

COMMITTEE

On MANUFACTURES and COMMERCE.

Sir John Riggs Miller, Bart.
Richard Atwood, Eſq;
Joſeph Harford, Eſq;
William Provis, Eſq;
Gaisford Gibbs, Eſq;
Samuel Cam, Eſq;
J. Gale Everit, Eſq;
John Billingſley, Eſq;
William Whitaker, Eſq;
Daniel Lyſons, M. D.
Mr. Robert Meares
James Sutton, Eſq;
Charles Hamilton, Eſq;
Simeon Moreau, Eſq;
John Anſtie, Eſq;
Rev. Dr. Cleobury
William Croſely, Eſq;
Mr. John Newman
Mr. John Lediard
Mr. Iſaac Collett
Mr. Jonathan Noad
Mr. William Evill
Mr. Bethell, *Bradford*
Mr. William Clark

COMMITTEE

On MECHANICKS and the USEFUL ARTS.

Sir John Riggs Miller, Bart.
W. Falconer, M. D. F. R. S.
William Watſon, Eſq;
Mr. William Evill
A. Fothergill, M. D. F. R. S.
Mr. R. Cruttwell
*Rev. Mr. Hawes
Thomas Davis, Eſq;
William Whitaker, Eſq;
Daniel Lyſons, M. D.
Mr. Lionel Bretton
Mr. Samuel Hazard
John Gale Everit, Eſq;
Mr. Robert Meares
Mr. T. Bonnor, *artiſt*
Charles Hamilton, Eſq:
Mr. William Clark
William Clavill, Eſq;
Rev. Mr. Barter
Mr. George Winter
Mr. Joſiah Hazard
Mr. Henry Murrell
Mr. Laurence Fielde, *architect.*

COMMITTEE

Of CORRESPONDENCE and ENQUIRY.

Sir John Riggs Miller, Bart.
*Dr. Joſ. Prieſtley, F. R. S.
*Dr. Hunter, *York*
William Falconer, M. D. F. R. S.
William Watſon, Eſq;
*Sir Thomas Beevor, Bart.
C. H. Parry, M. D.
A. Fothergill, M. D. F. R. S.
Luck Anningſon, Eſq;
T. William Coke, Eſq;
*Mr. B. Pryce, *Saliſbury*
Wm. Whitaker, Eſq;
W. A. Ballard, Eſq;
*Simeon Moreau, Eſq;
*Mr. Richard Phillips
William Barwis, M. D.
*Mr. James Beeſly, *London*
*Arthur Young, Eſq;
James Stephens, Eſq;
*Rev. H. J. Cloſe
Mr. R. Cruttwell
Charles Hamilton, Eſq;
Alex. de Salis, Eſq;
*Jas. Anderſon, Eſq; LL. D. F. S. A. S.
Mr. George Winter
Daniel Lyſons, M. D.
John Anſtie, Eſq;
Rev. Dr. Cleobury
Rev. Mr. Randolph
Dr. Frazer
Mr. Matthew Randall
Mr. William Clark

Thoſe marked * are Honorary Members.

COMMITTEE

Of Books.

W. Falconer, M. D. F. R. S.	Edward Harington, Esq;
A. Fothergill, M. D. F. R. S.	Mr. R. Cruttwell
William Clavill, Esq;	Rev. Dr. Cleobury
Rev. Thomas Broughton	John Billingsley, Esq;
Mr. William Clark	William Crosely, Esq;
Mr. Josiah Hazard	Rev. Mr. Smith
William Whitaker, Esq;	W. A. Ballard, Esq.

N. *B.* Any three Members of either Committee to be a Quorum.

RULES

P R E M I U M S

ALPHABETICALLY ARRANGED.

	Page
ASH, planting Bogs with	31
Agriculture, Improvements in	33
Apple-Trees and Cyder	41
Ditto for Ditto	44
Buck-Wheat, ſowing of	27
Broad-Clover, ſubſtitute for	39
Bulls, for Stock	42
Beer, unwholeſome Ingredients in	49
Bees, greateſt Stock of	51
Ditto Honey and Wax, without deſtroying them	*ib.*
Carrots	27
Corn Crops, beſt and cleaneſt	28
Crops, beſt Courſe of	*ib.*
Calves without Milk, Rearing of	30
Cabbages, Scotch	34
Crab Stocks for Grafting	35
Cottagers, Induſtry in	36
Crab-Stocks in Hedges, planting of	44
Cyder of various Sorts	45
Combing Wool, beſt Mode of	48
Cement for Ciſterns	49
Coal-Mines, deſtroying Vapours in	*ib.*
Certificates, Forms of	53
Ditto	54
Ditto	55
Drill-Plough and Horſe-Hoe, uſe of	33
Drilling Wheat and Barley	39
Drill-Plough, beſt Invention of	49
Experiments, Courſe of	32
Eſſays, on ſundry Subjects	38
Fallows, Summer, extinction of	*ib.*
Flax, raiſing of	47
Floating Paſture Lands, Machine for	50
Fire, ſecuring Buildings from	51
Friendly Societies	*ib.*
Grubs in Land, deſtroying of	31
Goggly Sheep, cure of	34
Graſſes, repairing a failing Crop of	40
Ditto, natural	43
Green Winter Crops, machine for	49
Huſbandry, experiments in	32
Horſes for Cart	42
Hemp, raiſing of	47
Hand-Mill	50
Inſtruments, improved for cutting Graſs or Corn	28
Induſtry among Labourers	33
Killing Cattle, Italian method of	50

Lime

INDEX to the PREMIUMS.

	Page
Lime or Soaper's Aſhes, beſt mode of uſing	29
Liming, chalking, or marling Land	36
Men-Servants, good behaviour in	32
Manuring	38
Manure, vegetable	39
Mangel-Wurzel, property and uſes of	41
Malt-making	46
Madder, raiſing of	47
Norfolk-Plough	35
Neat Cattle uſed in Huſbandry	40
Potatoes, raiſing of	28
—— curled diſeaſe in	34
Preſerving Turnips and Cabbages in Winter	*ib.*
Plough, double-furrowed, uſing of	36
Potatoes, planting of	38
Parſnips as Food for Cattle	39
Potatoes, beſt way of uſing in fattening Hogs	41
Pigs, rearing of	43
Paper, writing and package, making of	46
Plough with two Horſes or four Oxen	48
Plough for Potatoe Crops	50
Ploughing, Premiums for	52
Rape-Seed for Oil	29
Reſervoirs in Farm-yards	31
Reaping by Women	36
Ram Lambs	42
Rape, tranſplanting	43
Sainfoin, raiſing of	27
Sheep-Downs, recovering worn-out by burn-beaking	36
Soils, conſtituent parts of rich and poor	37
Sheep, rot in	*ib.*
Stock, general	41
Smut in Wheat	45
Sheep-Marking	46
Steam Corn-Mill	48
Smoke in Glaſs-Houſes, deſtroying of	50
Turnips for Autumn Feeding	25
—— for Spring ditto	*ib.*
—— Hoeing of	26
—— deſtroying Fly on	*ib.*
Turnip-Rooted Cabbage, raiſing of	30
Thorn, white, for Quick-Hedges	31
Tithes, compenſation for	37
Timber Trees	43
Vetch, yellow-bloſſomed	30
Wheat, ſetting	26
Women-Servants, good behaviour in	32
Walnuts, Cheſnuts, and Beech, raiſing of	40
Weld or Woad	47
Wool, machine for winding of	48

RULES and ORDERS

OF THE

SOCIETY.

I.

THAT the Meetings of this Society ſhall be held as follows: On the ſecond Tueſday in the months of February, April, June, September, and November, at eleven o'clock in the forenoon, at the Society's Room in *Hetling-Houſe*, BATH;—that the *Annual Meeting* be held on the ſecond Tueſday in December, at the ſame hour, at the ſaid Room;—and that no new laws or rules ſhall be made, or the following altered, except by the *Annual Meeting*, which ſhall not conſiſt of leſs than fiſteen members.

II.

THAT the Preſident, or, in his abſence, one of the Vice-Preſidents, ſhall preſide at, and regulate, the debates of all general meetings; that the Vice-Preſidents ſhall take the chair by rotation, and that they ſhall be members of all Committees.

III. THAT

III.

That the Prefident, Vice-Prefidents, and all Committees, fhall be chofen at the Annual Meeting in December; and the faid Committees fhall be impowered to adjourn from time to time, as they may fee occafion: And that on any vacancy or vacancies (by death, removal, or refignation) being declared to the Secretary, he fhall make report thereof to the next general meeting, which fhall fill up fuch vacancy or vacancies in Committees, by appointing any other member or members, if neceffary.

IV.

That each Committee, when met, fhall choofe a Chairman, and enter minutes of their proceedings in a book for that purpofe. That all reports to the Society be made in writing, and figned by the Chairman; and that the Secretary fhall enter thofe reports in the Committee-book, or the Society's journal.

V.

That the meeting in November fhall be for preparing the bufinefs neceffary to come before the Annual Meeting; and that the bufinefs tranfacted at that Meeting fhall be, The appointment of officers; revifing and confirming, or amending, the conftitutional rules of the Society; the determination of Premiums claimed, and of New Premiums

for

for the year enſuing. That no alteration in the conſtitutional rules ſhall take place, unleſs propoſals for ſuch alteration be made at, and approved by, the laſt general meeting in November. And that no debate on ſuch alterations as come ſo recommended, or on the Premiums propoſed, ſhall take place; but on the queſtion being put at the Annual Meeting, they ſhall be agreed to, or negatived by vote.

VI.

THAT an annual ſubſcription of any ſum not leſs than one guinea, ſhall entitle a perſon to be a member; and that the names of all perſons who give annual benefactions, not leſs than half-a-guinea, ſhall be publiſhed with the liſt of members. That a benefaction, not leſs than twelve guineas, ſhall entitle any perſon to be a member for life. *And that every perſon, who has given or may give in his name as a member, is and ſhall be deemed ſuch, and his ſubſcription be conſidered as juſtly due to the Society, until he give notice in writing to the Secretary of his intention to withdraw it.*

VII.

THAT a liſt of ſuch premiums as the Society may think fit to offer, ſhall be printed and publiſhed on or before the firſt of February in every year; which premiums ſhall be claſſed under the ſeveral heads propoſed to be encouraged by this inſtitution.

VIII.

That no premium ſhall be offered to the public, until it has been firſt propoſed to and approved by a Committee, and agreed to by the Annual Meeting. And no premium or bounty ſhall be given to any candidate, unleſs the Society, at the Annual Meeting, ſhall be ſatisfied that ſuch candidate deſerves it.

IX.

That in order to excite emulation, and increaſe the number of competitors, no perſon ſhall receive a premium for a ſimilar crop, experiment, or improvement, more than once in ſeven years, or more than one premium in the ſame claſs in any one year.

X.

No member of the Society, who is a candidate for any premium or bounty, ſhall ſit in any Committee to which ſuch matters may be referred, or be preſent while the ſubject is under conſideration; nor ſhall ſuch candidate be preſent in the meetings of the Society, during the time the matter is before them, whether in debate, or for determination, unleſs when called in to anſwer ſuch queſtions as may be put to him.

XI.

That all claims for premiums or bounties ſhall be made at leaſt two months before the annual meeting in December, except ſuch as are otherwiſe

wiſe directed in the premium book. And that ſuch claims muſt be given in to the Secretary in writing, and be by him preſented to the next meeting of the Committee to which they relate.

XII.

In order that all rewards may be diſtributed with the utmoſt impartiality and juſtice, the Society ſhall, when they think it neceſſary, deſire the aſſiſtance of ſuch gentlemen, manufacturers, artiſts, or others, (though not members) as ſhall be deemed beſt able to judge of and diſcover the merits of any invention or improvement for which a premium is claimed.

XIII.

That premiums ſhall be both honorary and pecuniary; but that no premium or bounty ſhall be given by this Society to any perſon who ſhall have obtained a premium or bounty for the ſame invention, crop, or improvement, from this or any other Society.

XIV.

THAT as the principal deſign of this inſtitution is, by exciting a ſpirit of induſtry and ingenuity, to promote the public good, the Premiums offered ſhall be more immediately directed to improvements in agriculture, planting, and ſuch manufactures and arts as are beſt adapted to theſe counties.

XV. THAT

XV.

That ſome premiums be annually offered for the encouragement of induſtry and good behaviour amongſt ſervants in huſbandry, and labourers, in each of the four counties.

XVI.

That the Society's caſh ſhall be accounted for at the annual meeting in each year.

XVII.

That all drafts upon the Treaſurer ſhall be drawn at the general meeting, and ſigned by the Chairman, and two other members preſent.

XVIII.

That forty pounds be continued in the Secretary's hands, to anſwer any demands upon the Society between the general meetings; and on the auditing his accounts, if he has more than forty pounds in hand, he ſhall pay the ſurplus to the Treaſurer; if he has leſs than forty pounds in hand, a draft on the Treaſurer ſhall be given him for the deficiency. The Treaſurers to be the two Banks in Milſom-ſtreet alternately, one year each.

XIX.

That in order to encourage the ſtudy, as well as the practice of agriculture, &c. &c. honorary premiums ſhall be offered for the beſt-written

and

and most useful original essay on any of the subjects to which the views of this Society may be extended, that may be sent to their meetings; the Society to give out the subjects in their annual list of premiums: and that such essays as shall be approved at the annual meeting, be printed and published at the expence of the Society. Every member to have one copy, and the rest of the impression to be sold, and the profits applied to the Society's use; unless the author shall think proper to print the same at his own expence, or the annual meeting shall otherwise direct.

XX.

THAT the authors of such essays shall send them sealed to the Secretary without a name, but with some mark corresponding with another mark on the outside of an inclosed sealed-up paper, in which their names are written: That such essays as are rejected shall be left in the Secretary's hands, and if they are not called for, shall be destroyed at the succeeding annual meeting.

XXI.

A candidate for a premium, or a person applying for a bounty, being detected in any attempt to impose on the Society, shall not only forfeit such premium or bounty, but be declared incapable of obtaining any for the future.

XXII.

THAT the Secretary ſhall procure all ſuch books and ſtationary ware as are needful for the Society's uſe, and keep fair accounts of all monies received and diſburſed by him: The ſaid accounts to be ſettled and balanced at each meeting in the Society's caſh-book, when a Committee of Accounts ſhall be appointed to audit them. He ſhall alſo perform the neceſſary buſineſs of his office with diligence and integrity, viz.—Attend all meetings and committees of the Society;—make all minutes and reſolutions, and enter them fairly in the Journal or Committee books;—read all letters and other papers ſent to the Society, and prepare ſuch anſwers thereto as the Society ſhall direct; and preſerve or record regularly in the book of correſpondence ſuch as are worthy of preſervation;—ſign all publications, notices, and receipts;—and attend to the printing of whatever the Society may direct to be printed, and correct the preſs. He ſhall alſo collect ſubſcriptions, and viſit manufactories, or apply for particular information reſpecting them when required by the Society ſo to do;—and as much as poſſible make himſelf acquainted with the various Arts, &c. &c. to which the views of the Society ſhall be directed. He ſhall alſo regularly enter the minutes, proceedings, and reſolutions, of each meeting, for the inſpection of the next:——And in conſideration of his trouble, and the

the close attention he must give to this business, he shall be allowed an annual salary.

XXIII.

That on any emergency, the Secretary, with the concurrence of five members signified in writing, and signed with their names, may call an extra general meeting by advertisement in the public papers of the respective counties: And in case of the death of the Secretary, three Vice-Presidents shall be authorized to call an extra general meeting in like manner; which extra general meeting shall be competent to the appointment of a person to act as Secretary till the next annual meeting.

XXIV.

All letters relative to the business of the Society, being laid by the Secretary before the Committee of Correspondence, that Committee shall be at liberty from time to time to refer such letters as they think proper to the other respective Committees, without waiting to report them to a meeting of the Society; unless such letters relate to the granting any new premium or bounty.

XXV.

All the books, papers, and correspondence, of the Society shall remain under the care of the Secretary, to be inspected by the members at any reasonable time.

XXVI.

All models of machines and implements, which ſhall have obtained premiums or bounties, ſhall be the property of the Society, and be kept in their rooms for the inſpection of farmers, manufacturers, &c.

XXVII.

As the proper and regular diſpatch of buſineſs at the General Meetings will very much depend on the diligence and attention of the ſeveral Committees; it is reſpectfully requeſted, that the Gentlemen appointed thereon will give as general attendance as poſſible, both at the ſittings of Committees, when ſummoned, and alſo at the meetings of the Society, and meet as nearly as they can to the hours appointed.

XXVIII.

In caſe any perſon ſhall be diſpoſed to leave a ſum of money to this Society by will, the following form is offered for that purpoſe:

Item, I give and bequeath to A. B. and C. D. the ſum of pounds, upon condition, and to the intent, that they pay the ſame to the Treaſurer or Secretary for the time being, of a Society inſtituted at Bath 1777, who call themſelves "The Society for the Encouragement of "Agriculture, Arts, Manufactures, and Com-"merce;"

" merce;" which ſaid ſum of pounds I will and deſire may be paid out of my perſonal eſtate, and applied towards carrying on the laudable deſigns of the ſaid Society.

XXIX.

FORM *of a* LETTER *to a Gentleman whoſe Subſcription is in Arrear.*

" SIR,

" I am directed to inform you, that your annual ſubſcription of has been in arrear ſince the day of : And as it is of conſequence for the Society to know what ſums of money they can beſtow in premiums, you are reſpectfully deſired to order the payment of it to the Secretary.

" By order of the Society,

" WM. MATTHEWS, Secretary.

N. B. New Editions of the Four Volumes of the Society's Select Papers, lately publiſhed, may be had of Mr. Cruttwell, printer, in Bath; Mr. Dilly, bookſeller, London; or by giving orders to any bookſeller in the kingdom.

Order of Proceedings at the Meetings.

I.

THE books of rules and orders, of minutes and correfpondence, fhall be laid on the table, before the Prefident or Vice-Prefident; the Secretary fitting at his right hand.

II.

None but members to be admitted to the meetings of the Society, without leave firft obtained of the faid meetings.

III.

When any Member fpeaks, he fhall addrefs himfelf to the Chair; and if two Members fpeak together, the prefiding member fhall call them to order, and decide which fhall fpeak firft.

IV.

When any matter is in debate, if a member fhall fpeak to new bufinefs, the prefiding member fhall call him to order.

V.

No debate fhall be entered into, or queftion put, on any motion, unlefs that motion be feconded.

VI.

No motion that has been rejected fhall be made again in the fame meeting.

VII. That

VII.

That in meetings of Committees the ſame order be obſerved as in the third article of the order of proceedings in meetings of the Society.

VIII.

At all meetings of the Society, buſineſs ſhall be tranſacted in the following order:—

1*ſt*. The meeting to be conſtituted by entering the names of the members preſent.

2*dly*. Minutes of the preceding meeting to be read, and reports of Committees to be received.

3*dly*. Accounts ſince the preceding meeting to be audited, balanced, and ſigned by the Chairman.

4*thly*. Correſpondence to be read, and referred to the reſpective Committees.

5*thly*. New matter to be offered on the ſeveral ſubjects in ſucceſſion.

PREMIUMS

OFFERED BY

THE BATH SOCIETY,

JANUARY, 1790.

To the PUBLICK.

Society's Rooms, Bath, Dec. 9th, 1789.

THE Society for the encouragement of Agriculture, Arts, Manufactures, and Commerce, in the Counties of *Somerset*, *Wilts*, *Glocester*, and *Dorset*, propose, in pursuance of their plan, to bestow the following Premiums:

CLASS I.

PREMIUMS *for Agriculture, Planting, the Increase of Live Stock, and Industry in Servants.*

1. *Turnips for Autumn Feeding.*—To the person who shall raise the greatest weight of the red, white, or green Turnips per acre, on the greatest number of acres, in proportion to the quantity and quality of his arable land, for Fall Feeding, the said crop to be twice hoed; a Silver Cup, value Five Guineas.

Claim to be made, and the crop viewed, before the meeting in November 1790.

2. *Turnips for Spring Feeding.*—To the person who shall raise, in proportion to the quantity and quality of his arable land, the greatest weight per acre, on the greatest number of acres, of the red, white, or green Round Turnips, twice hoed, for Spring Feeding; a Silver Cup, value Five Guineas.

For the next greatest quantity, on farms of not more than 50l. a year, Three Guineas, or a Piece of Plate of equal value.

Claims to be made, the crops viewed, and certificates of the weight per acre, and number of acres, to be produced, at or before the Society's meeting in March 1790.

3. *Hoeing*

3. *Hoeing Turnips.*—To the labouring man who ſhall hand-hoe the greateſt quantity of Turnips in one ſeaſon, not leſs than five acres, in a workmanlike manner, Three Guineas.

N. B. The ſaid labourer to be an inhabitant of, and reſiding in one of the four counties. All claimants muſt deliver in their claims, with their names and places of abode, the number of acres hoed, and the ſort of hoe uſed, certified by the maſters for whom they worked, and the miniſter and churchwardens of the pariſhes where the work was done, to the Secretary, on or before the firſt of November 1790.

A premium of One Guinea will alſo be given to the Woman who hoes the greateſt quantity, not leſs than three acres.

4. *For deſtroying the Fly on Turnips.*—To the perſon who ſhall diſcover, and make known an effectual remedy for deſtroying the Fly on Turnips, to be fully aſcertained by repeated experiments, on or before the firſt day of November, 1790; Ten Guineas, or a Silver Cup of the ſame value.

5. *Setting Wheat.*—To the farmer who ſhall ſet, either by hand or drill-plough, and keep clean by hoeing, the greateſt quantity of land, not leſs than ten acres, with Wheat, in autumn 1790, the produce to be not leſs than thirty buſhels per acre; Five Guineas, or a Silver Cup of the ſame value.

Certificates of the quantity of land ſet, and the produce per acre, with a fair ſample, containing not leſs than one buſhel of the ſaid wheat, to be produced at the Society's meeting, on or before November 1790.

N. B. As ſetting wheat is now generally practiſed in Norfolk with the greateſt ſucceſs, the Norfolk method is recommended. The farmers there generally ſet their wheat on a clover lay of one year, on one ploughing. They drill two rows of holes on the earth turned out of the furrow; the rows four inches apart, and the holes in each row three inches diſtant, and drop two grains in each hole, but none in the furrows; two pecks and one quarter of ſeed will ſet an acre, and the expence of ſetting is now from five to ten ſhillings.

Any

Any perſon who wiſhes for more particular information relative to this excellent method, may have it by applying to the Secretary; or by referring to the Society's *firſt Volume of Select Papers*, or to the *Farmer's Magazine* for Dec. 1777, in which a clear and explicit deſcription of the method uſed by the beſt Norfolk farmers is inſerted.

6. *French or Buck Wheat.*—To the perſon who, in May 1790, ſhall ſow the greateſt quantity, not leſs than ten acres, with French or Buck-Wheat, and the following autumn ſow or plant the ſame land with Wheat; the produce of Wheat to be not leſs than thirty buſhels to an acre; a Silver Cup value Five Guineas.

All claimants to produce certificates of the quantity of land ſown, the nature of the ſoil, and the produce of both crops per acre, on or before the firſt of November 1790.

7. *Sainfoin, or French Graſs.*—To the perſon who, between the firſt of January 1790 and 1791, ſhall ſow and cultivate the greateſt quantity of land, not leſs than thirty acres, with Sainfoin; Ten Guineas, or a Silver Cup of the ſame value. This graſs is particularly recommended on chalky or rocky ſoil.

The nature of the ſoil, the quantity of ſeed ſown per acre, the mode of tillage, and the average produce of the crop, to be properly certified to the Society, at or before the September meeting 1791, and timely notice given for the ſaid crop to be viewed by the Society's Inſpector, if required.

N. B. This premium is reſtricted to pariſhes where Sainfoin has not been uſually raiſed.

8. *Carrots.*—To the Farmer who, in the year 1790, ſhall ſow the greateſt quantity of land, not leſs than five acres, with Carrots, and produce the largeſt, cleaneſt, and beſt crop; Five Guineas, or a Silver Cup of that value.

Claims to be made, and certificates ſpecifying the nature of the land, and the quantity of buſhels on each acre, to be produced at the Society's meeting in November 1790.

To

To the perſon (not being a gardener) who ſhall raiſe the next largeſt quantity, not leſs than two acres; Three Guineas.

9. *Beſt and cleaneſt Crops of Corn.*—To the Farmer who, in proportion to the quantity and quality of his land, ſhall in the year 1790, in a general point of view, exhibit the beſt Crops of Corn, Pulſe, Roots, Graſſes, &c. and whoſe Farm, in reſpect of fertility, cleanneſs, fences, &c. ſhall be found in the moſt complete order; Ten Guineas, or a Piece of Plate of equal value.

Claims to be made on or before the firſt of April. The Crops of Graſſes, &c. to be viewed in May or June; and the Corn, Pulſe, Roots, &c. in Auguſt 1790.

N. B. The claimants to be at the expence of the Inſpectors viewing their reſpective crops.

10. *Improved Inſtruments for cutting Graſs or Corn.*—To the perſon who ſhall make the greateſt improvement in the inſtrument now uſed for cutting Graſs or Corn Crops; or who ſhall make the beſt inſtrument for thoſe purpoſes, on a new and ſimple conſtruction; Five Guineas, or a Silver Cup of equal value.

One of the ſaid inſtruments to be ſent to the Society on or before the firſt of July 1790.

11. *Beſt Courſe of Crops.*—To the perſon who, from actual experiments made by himſelf, ſhall aſcertain a Courſe of Crops, either on light or heavy land, which during ſeven years ſhall prove moſt profitable, and leave the land in the beſt ſtate; Ten Guineas.

A general account of the Crops to be atteſted and ſent with each claim to the Society on or before the firſt of June 1796.

12. *Raiſing Potatoes.*—To the Farmer, not renting or holding more than forty pounds per annum, and who, not having heretofore cultivated Potatoes for ſale, ſhall raiſe the beſt and greateſt crop at the leaſt expence, on the greateſt quantity, not leſs than two acres of land; Five Guineas, or a Piece of Plate of that value.

Claims

Claims, with a fair sample of not less than a bushel of the said Potatoes, to be sent to the Society on or before the first of November 1790, and affidavits of the quantity of land and produce per acre.

To one Cottager in each of the four counties, not renting more than forty shillings per annum, nor having less than five children, who in the year 1790 shall raise on his own garden-plot the greatest quantity, not less than thirty bushels, of good Potatoes; One Guinea.

Claims, with an account of the quantity raised, signed by the claimant, and attested by his master, and the overseer of the parish, to be sent on or before the first Tuesday in November 1790.

13. *Best Mode of applying Lime or Soaper's Ashes.*—To the person who, from his own experiments actually made, or which he may make during the years 1790 and 1791, shall ascertain and point out the best mode and time for applying Lime or Soaper's Ashes as a manure on Pasture Land, and give an explicit account of its operation and success; Five Guineas, or a Silver Cup of equal value.

The number of acres, the quantity of Lime or Ashes laid on each acre, the value of the land before and after such manuring, and a fair estimate of the expence, to be sent in, attested, at or before the Society's meeting in September 1792.

14. *Rape-Seed for Oil.*—Five Guineas, or a Silver Cup of equal value, will be given to the person, who (not having heretofore cultivated Rape) shall raise the greatest quantity, not less than twenty-four bushels of seed per acre, on the greatest number of acres, not less than ten. The Oil to be extracted from the said seed, and to be used in the woollen manufactory.

The crops to be viewed when the seed is nearly ripe; and a fair sample of not less than a peck of the said seed to be sent with each claim, on or before the first of September 1791.——N. B. Genuine seed may be had by applying to the Secretary.

15. *Turnip-*

15. *Turnip-Rooted Cabbage.*—To the person who, in the year 1790, shall, in proportion to the quantity and quality of his arable land, raise on the greatest quantity, not less than three acres, the best and heaviest crop of Turnip-rooted Cabbage, for Spring Feed; Five Guineas, or a Silver Cup of that value.

Timely notice to be given for the crop to be viewed; and claims to be made in February or March 1791.

16. *Rearing Calves without Milk.*—To the Farmer who, from January 1790 to January 1791, shall rear the greatest number of Calves, not less than five, without Milk, and who shall discover to the Society the best and cheapest method of so rearing them; a Silver Cup value Six Guineas.

The Calves which have been so reared to be viewed by the Society's Inspectors at ten months old.

17. *Liming, Chalking, or Marling Land.*—That a Silver Cup, value Five Guineas, be given to the farmer who shall, in proportion to the extent of his land, lime, chalk, or marle, the greatest quantity, not less than five acres, of down-land, sheep-walk, or other pasture land, with intent to remain as pasture, giving an account of the quantity laid on per acre, the expence, and the improvement thereby.

N. B. As the improvement will not be fully known in less than four years, claims are to be made at the meeting in September 1793.

18. *The Yellow-blossomed Vetch.*—To the person who shall make and report the most satisfactory experiments on the Lathyrus Pratensis, commonly called the Yellow-blossomed Perennial Vetch, or the Bush Vetch; sown upon not less than two acres of ground, tending to its introduction as an article of common husbandry; Five Guineas.

N. B. This is not intended to preclude the continued cultivation of the *Blue Vetch*, for any new and valuable experiments in the growth and use of which, the same premium is hereby offered.

The crops to be viewed, and claims to be made, at or before the Society's meeting in September 1790.

19. *Raising*

19. *Raising White-Thorn for Quick-Hedges.*—To the person (not being a gardener or nursery-man) who, in the years 1790 and 1791, shall raise from the haws the greatest quantity, not less than a hundred thousand, of White-Thorn Plants for Quick-Hedges, and keep the same clean from weeds till they are of a size proper for transplanting; Five Guineas.

A certificate to be produced of the quantity of haws sown, the time of sowing, and number of the plants; and claim made, at or before the Society's meeting in October 1794. The plantation to be viewed by the Society's Inspectors.

20. *Planting Bogs with Ash.*—To the person who shall, at his own charge, raise or plant the largest quantity of boggy land with Ash, either for timber or underwood; the land planted to be not less than one acre, and the number of plants per acre to be not less than three thousand if planted, or six thousand if sown; Five Guineas.

Claims to be made, and the plantation viewed by the Society's Inspectors, on or before September 1792.

21. *Destroying Grubs in Land.*—To the person who shall discover, and communicate to the Society, a method of destroying those large Grey Grubs, in pasture and arable land, from which proceeds the Cock-Chaffer-Beetle, that shall, on experiment, be found the easiest, most effectual, and least prejudicial to the grass or other produce of such lands; Ten Guineas, or a Silver Cup of like value.

A certificate, proving that the means used have been successful, to be produced, and claim to be made, at or before the Society's meeting in November 1790.

22. *Reservoirs in Farm-Yards.*—To the Farmer, who, in the year 1790, shall make and secure from leakage, in the cheapest and most effectual manner, the best Reservoir in his barton for the reception of water from his dung-heaps, stables, hog-sties and cow-house, and carry the said water to his pasture lands as a manure; Five Guineas, or a Silver Cup of equal value.

Notice to be given that the Reservoir may be viewed by the Society's Inspectors in October; and claim to be made at the Society's meeting in November.

23. *Experiments*

23. *Experiments in Husbandry*—An honorary Premium of Plate will be given to the person who, on or before the first of November 1790, shall send to the Society a clear and explicit account of any experiment which he has himself made in husbandry, and which the Society shall think to be of an interesting nature.

N. B. This Premium is extended to accounts of Planting, and breeding or rearing Cattle.

24. *Course of Experiments.*—To the person who, from actual experiments made by himself during a course of seven years, shall prepare, and lay before the Society, the best comparative estimate of the success attending the Broadcast and Drill Husbandry, on the four grand divisions of soil, to wit, sand, loam, chalk, and clay, or either of them; fairly stating the expence of each through the usual course of crops, together with the nett produce, and profit or loss each year,—will be given such a reward as the said account may by able and proper judges be thought to merit, not exceeding Twenty Guineas. The said estimate to be given in at the Society's meeting in November 1796.

25. *Good Behaviour in Men-Servants.*—To one man-servant in each of the four counties, who having lived with a good character the greatest number of years, not less than five, shall continue to live five years longer in the same service, and produce at the end of that term a satisfactory certificate of such continued good behaviour; Three Guineas.

26. *Good Behaviour in Women-Servants.*—To one woman-servant in each of the four counties, who having lived with a good character in one place the greatest number of years, not less than five, shall continue to live five years longer in the same service, and produce at the end of that term a satisfactory certificate of such continued good behaviour; Three Guineas.

N. B. Certificates and notices, adapted to each of the foregoing descriptions of claimants, to be sent in before the first of November each year, according to the respective forms inserted next after the list of premiums.

27. *Industry.*

27. *Induſtry.*—To one labourer in huſbandry, in each of the four counties, not renting more than four pounds per annum, by whom the greateſt number, not leſs than ſeven, of his own legitimate children, have been brought up to at leaſt ſeven years of age in habits of honeſt induſtry; and who has not at any time received any relief or aſſiſtance from any pariſh or townſhip; Three Guineas.

To the labourer, as above-mentioned, who in like manner has brought up the next greateſt number, not leſs than five, of his own legitimate children; Two Guineas.

The above claims to be made on or before the firſt of November 1790, accompanied by a certificate according to the printed form.

28. *Improvements in Agriculture.*—An honorary Reward will be given to the perſon who ſhall write the beſt Eſſay on the Improvements in Agriculture, that have been ſucceſsfully introduced into this kingdom within theſe fifty years paſt. The ſaid Eſſay to be produced at or before the Society's meeting in September 1790.

29. *Uſe of the Drill-Plough and Horſe-Hoe.*—Complaints having been frequently made by Gentlemen Farmers, that their ſervants and labourers are ſo prejudiced againſt the uſe of New Drill-Ploughs, or improved implements in huſbandry, that they will often either not work them properly, or ſpoil them, in order that they may return to the uſe of thoſe commonly employed;—

A Premium of Two Guineas will be given to the ſervant or labourer in huſbandry, who in the year 1790 ſhall ſow with a Drill-Plough the greateſt number of acres, not leſs than twenty, with any kind of Grain, or with Turnip, Rape, Lucerne, Sainfoin, or other Seeds.

A Premium of One Guinea for the next greateſt number of acres ſo drilled, not leſs than twelve. Alſo,

A Premium of Two Guineas to the labourer who ſhall horſe-hoe the intervals or alleys between the rows of the greateſt number of acres ſo drilled, in the beſt manner.

Certificates of the number of acres drilled or horſe-hoed, and that the work is well done, ſigned by the maſter, to be produced at or before the Society's meeting in Sept. 1790.

The ſaid Premiums are extended to the year 1791.

30. *Cure of Goggly Sheep.*—To the perſon who, on or before the firſt of September 1790, ſhall communicate to the Society the moſt accurate deſcription, and beſt obſervations on the diſeaſe called the Goggles in Sheep, together with the moſt effectual remedy, aſcertained by ſucceſsful experiment on not leſs than twenty ſheep ſo diſeaſed, and produce a certificate or certificates of their cure from their owner or owners; Ten Guineas.

31. *Scotch Cabbages.*—To the perſon who, in proportion to the quantity and quality of his land, in the autumn of 1790, ſhall raiſe the beſt crop of Scotch Cabbages as food for cattle; Five Guineas.

The quantity of land planted not to be leſs than five acres. Claims to be made, and the crop viewed, on or before the 8th of February 1791.——The weight not to be leſs than twenty-five tons per acre.

32. *Curled Diſeaſe in Potatoes.*—To the perſon who ſhall diſcover the cauſe, and point out an effectual remedy for the Curled Diſeaſe in Potatoes, and communicate the ſame to the Society, with ſatisfactory proofs annexed, on or before the firſt of November 1790; Five Guineas, or a Silver Cup of like value.

33. *Preſerving Turnips and Cabbages in Winter.*—To the perſon who, on or before the firſt of September 1790, ſhall diſcover and communicate to the Society the cheapeſt and moſt effectual method of preſerving Turnips and Cabbages from froſt and rotting through the winter, as ſpring feed for cattle in the months of March and April; Five Guineas.

N. B. Specimens of the Turnips and Cabbages ſo preſerved, to be viewed by perſons appointed, or produced at the Society's meeting in April 1790.

34. *Norfolk Plough.*—To the Farmer who, in proportion to the quantity of his arable land, ſhall plough the greateſt number of acres, not leſs than twenty, with the Norfolk Plough, or any other that goes with a pair of horſes only, and without a driver; Five Guineas, or a Silver Cup of the ſame value.

For the next greateſt quantity will be given a plough proved capable of performing the work well, and recommended by this Society. Claims and atteſted certificates to be delivered in at or before the November meeting 1790.

N. B. Since the above Premium was agreed on, ſome perſons have very inconſiderately objected, that were the practice of ploughing without a driver to become general, there would ſoon be a want of ploughmen; very abſurdly ſuppoſing, that the boys who drive the horſes are thereby inſtructed to guide the plough.

But as a proof that this apprehenſion is perfectly groundleſs, it is a well-known fact, that in the counties of Norfolk, Suffolk, and Eſſex, where agriculture is carried to a higher pitch than in any other part of the kingdom, and where there are the greateſt number of the beſt ploughmen, there is not a ſingle inſtance to be ſeen of boys driving the horſes, or of more than a pair of horſes being uſed in a plough, even in land too wet and heavy to bear turnips.

If the farmers in the Weſt wiſh to have a ſucceſſion of good ploughmen, let them follow the example of the Norfolk Farmers, who very frequently give hats or buckſkin breeches to be ploughed for by ten or twelve young ploughmen, and by that means raiſe ſuch a ſpirit of emulation among them, that they far excel thoſe of other counties in this art.

35. *Raiſing Crab-Stocks for Grafting.*—To the perſon who ſhall, in the years 1790 and 1791, raiſe the greateſt number (not leſs than five thouſand) of Crab-Stocks from ſeed, and properly tranſplant the ſame, ſo that they ſhall be fit for grafting; Five Guineas, or a Piece of Plate of equal value.

And the ſame Premium to the perſon who ſhall graft not leſs than two thouſand of the ſaid Stocks with the beſt Cyder or Table fruit.

The plantations to be viewed at the proper ſeaſons, and claims to be made at or before the firſt of Auguſt 1794.

36. *Recovering Sheep-Downs worn out by Burn-Beaking.*—To the Farmer who ſhall, from actual experiment on not leſs than twenty acres, at or before the meeting in June 1790, point out the beſt and leaſt expenſive method of recovering Sheep-Downs that are worn out by the pernicious practice of Burn-beaking or Denſhiring; Five Guineas, or a Silver Cup of that value.

Certificates to be produced of the ſtate of the land previous to the beginning of the proceſs, and again on the Premium being claimed.

37. *Induſtry in Cottagers.*—To the Cottager, who is a day-labourer in huſbandry, with a family of not leſs than four children, (the eldeſt of whom ſhall not be more than twelve years old) who ſhall bring proof of their earnings, either in ſpinning or knitting, or both, from March 1790 to March 1791, given in on oath, with the age of each child ſo employed; and a certificate of their good characters from the Miniſter or Churchwardens where they reſide; Three Guineas.

Claims to be ſent in before the 10th of March 1791. The ſaid earnings not to be leſs than one penny per day under nine years old, and two-pence per day above that age.

38. *Women Reaping.*—To the woman who, in the harveſt of 1790, ſhall reap the greateſt number of acres (not leſs than five) of wheat, and perform the ſame in a huſbandlike manner; Two Guineas.

To the woman who ſhall reap the next greateſt number of acres, not leſs than four, in like manner; One Guinea.

Certificates of the work done, ſigned by the Maſter, to be ſent with claims on or before the firſt of October 1790.

39. *Double-Furrow Plough.*—Whereas the Double-Furrow Plough, uſed for ſome years paſt by John Billingſley, eſq; of Aſhwick-Grove, appears from long and conſtant experience to be the beſt for expediting and ſaving of labour

and

and expence, and for performing the work well, of any yet conſtructed;—the coſt of the ſaid plough will be given as a Premium to the Farmer who ſhall introduce, and plough therewith the greateſt number of acres in the years 1790 and 1791.

Claims to be made, accompanied with affidavits, at or before the meeting in March 1792.

N. B. This plough turns two acres in a day with three horſes, or four oxen, and without a driver.

A Premium of Five Guineas will alſo be given for the beſt Double-Furrow Plough on a new conſtruction.

40. *Conſtituent parts of rich and poor Soils.*—For aſcertaining the conſtituent parts of a very rich Soil, and of a very poor one, by ſuitable experiments, in order to determine what principles are wanting in the latter, or, in other words, what ought to be added to it, or how altered to meliorate it, and render it equal to the former; an Honorary Premium.

Claims to be made at or before the meeting in November 1790.

41. *Rot in Sheep.*—The liver diſeaſe, termed the Rot in Sheep, being now generally allowed to proceed from the ova of an aquatic inſect, vulgarly called the FLUKE; an Honorary Premium will be given for the beſt account of its genus and ſpecies, the plant which it inhabits, and the beſt method of extirpating this inſect, or preventing its deſtructive effects in the animal œconomy.

42. *Compenſation for Tithes.*—The Society being convinced, that the payment of Tithes in kind tends not only to ſow diſſention between the Clergy and their Pariſhioners, but is certainly a very great hindrance to improvements in Agriculture; and it being much to be wiſhed that the matter may be taken up in a national view; an Honorary Premium of Plate will be given for the beſt Eſſay on the moſt practicable mode of giving an equitable Compenſation for Tithes in general throughout the kingdom.

The Eſſays to be ſent to the Secretary on or before the firſt day of October 1790.

43. *Essays.*—A Piece of Plate will be given as an Honorary Premium to the person who shall, before the first day of September 1790, write and present to the Society, the best, most useful, and approved Essay, on either of the following subjects, from experiments actually made:—

1st. On the art of making Butter and Cheese, pointing out the real causes of the defects we frequently find in each, and the best practical preventatives.

2dly. On the management of Grass Lands in general, distinguishing the proper treatment of each soil, &c.

3dly. On the best and most approved method of laying down worn-out arable.

4thly. For an account of the best Course of Experiments to ascertain the comparative value of Butter and Cheese; viz. BUTTER from new milk alone, from half new milk and half whey, and from whey alone. CHEESE from new milk, from half-skimm'd milk, and from skimm'd milk only.

All the above Essays to be written from experiments actually made.

44. *Extinction of Summer Fallows.*—A Premium of Five Guineas, or a Piece of Plate, will be given to the person who, in the course of seven years, shall determine how far the total extinction of Summer Fallows on light land may be practised with success.

The same experiment to be made on heavy lands.

Claims to be made at or before the Sept. meeting 1796.

45. *Manuring.*—For manuring the greatest quantity of light Sandy Land with Clay, not less than ten acres, nor less than sixty cart loads, of thirty bushels each, of clay to be laid on per acre; Five Guineas, or a Silver Cup of that value.

Claims, with an account of the success, to be made on or before the first of September 1791.

46. *Planting Potatoes.*—To the person who, from experiments actually made, shall discover whether whole Potatoes, or Cuttings, are to be preferred in planting; and if whole, of what size; a Silver Cup, value Three Guineas. The quantity

tity or weight planted per acre, in both methods, muſt be ſpecified, and claims made at or before the meeting in November 1790.

47. *Vegetable Manure.*—To the Farmer who, in the year 1790, ſhall plough in the greateſt quantity of Clover, Buck-Wheat, Vetches, &c. by way of Manure, on the greateſt number of acres not leſs than ten, and report the ſucceſs thereof to the Society's meeting in November 1791; Three Guineas, or a piece of Plate to the ſame amount.

N. B. This is particularly recommended to the occupiers of heavy land.

48. *Parſnips as a Food for Cattle.*—To the Farmer who, in the year 1790, ſhall on the greateſt quantity, not leſs than two acres of land, raiſe the greateſt weight of Parſnips per acre, as a food for Neat Cattle, Sheep, or Swine; and thereby aſcertain their real and comparative value with carrots, turnips, or potatoes; and report fully and explicitly on the ſubject, at or before the meeting in June 1791; Five Guineas, or a Piece of Plate of equal value. Claims to be then made.

49. *Drilled Wheat and Barley.*—To the Farmer who ſhall, in the years 1790 and 1791, raiſe the greateſt crop of Drilled Wheat or Barley in a comparative experiment with Broad-caſt on the ſame land, and render an accurate account of the expences; each crop to be not leſs than two acres; a Silver Cup, value Five Guineas.

Claims to be made on or before the firſt of November 1791, with affidavits of the quantity per acre, &c. &c.

50. *Subſtitute for Broad Clover.*—A Premium of Five Guineas, or Plate of equal value, will be given to the perſon who, in the years 1790 or 1791, ſhall introduce and make known to the Society the beſt ſubſtitute for Broad Clover, (Saintfoin excepted) or who ſhall by actual experiments diſcover in what manner lands on which broad clover has of late years generally failed, may be managed ſo as to admit of that plant being again cultivated thereon with ſucceſs.

Claims to be made at or before the firſt of Nov. 1791.

51. *Raiſing*

51. *Raising Walnuts, Chesnuts, and Beech.*—A Premium of Five Guineas, or a Silver Cup, will be given to the person who shall, before January 1798, plant, and effectually fence in and secure, the greatest number, not less than two acres, with Walnut, Chesnut, or Beech Trees, on lands generally left waste, or appropriated to Firs only.

The plantations to be viewed, and claims made in April, four years after planting, with an account of the number of plants per acre, and the whole expence attending the plantation to that time.

52. *Neat Cattle used in Husbandry.*—To the Gentleman or Farmer, who shall, in the years 1790 or 1791, plough with Oxen, or with Oxen and Bulls, or any Neat Cattle, collared and harnessed, the greatest number of acres, (in proportion to his arable land) not less than one hundred, and shall constantly use such oxen, &c. through one whole year, in the different departments of Husbandry, and give the Society an accurate account of the year's expence attending them; together with his calculation of the advantages or disadvantages attending the working of such team, on a comparison with a team of horses, sufficient to have done the same business; Ten Guineas, or a Piece of Plate of equal value.

N. B. Bulls, Gales, and Spayed Heifers, are included in the above Premium.

☞ Two Guineas will be given to the driver.

Accounts to be sent, and claims to be made, on or before the first of November in either year.

53. *Repairing without re-ploughing a failing Crop of Grasses.*—To the Gentleman or Farmer who, in the years 1790 or 1791, shall produce to the Society the best account, founded on experiment, of repairing, without reploughing, a failing crop of Grasses, sown on land intended to be laid down for pasture; Five Guineas, or a Piece of Plate of equal value.

Claims to be made before the first day of November in either year.

54. *Propagation*

53. *Propagation and Uses of the Mangel-Wurzel.*—To the person who, in the years 1790 and 1791, shall most successfully propagate, by experiments on different soils, and by different methods of manuring and management, on not less than two acres, the plant called *Mangel-Wurzel*, or Root of Scarcity; whose plants shall be of the largest size; and who shall send to this Society the most clear and satisfactory account in writing, of the properties of this vegetable; together with its effects on a comparison with Turnips, Carrots, Parsnips and Cabbages, in feeding different kinds of cattle, in the winter and spring; Ten Guineas, or a Piece of Plate of equal value.

Claims to be made before the first of November in the years 1791 or 1792.

55. *Apple-Trees and Cyder.*—To the person who shall write and send to the Society, (under the usual regulations) before the meeting in June 1790, the best practical Essay, founded on experience, on raising Apple Stocks; the most successful method of Grafting, and the raising of Apple-Trees for the Orchard; together with the best Essay on gathering in apples, making them into Cyder, and of managing that cyder until it shall become fit for use; a Silver Cup, value Five Guineas.

56. *General Stock.*—To the person who shall satisfactorily describe at large, in an Essay which shall be deemed by the Committee proper for publication in the Society's next volume, those kinds of Oxen, Cows, and Sheep, most advantageous for general Stock, on large, middling, and small farms, divided into the most useful proportions of arable and pasture; on light, heavy, and damp soils; and both having, and not having, an extensive right of common in these Western counties; Five Guineas.

57. *Best Mode of using Potatoes in fattening Hogs.*—To the person who shall construct a cheap and durable Oven or Kiln for baking Potatoes for Hogs; and who, by repeated comparative experiments in 1790 and 1791, shall ascertain and fully impart in writing to this Society, the comparative advantages of fattening Hogs by these four methods:—

1. On

1. On boiled Potatoes alone.
2. On baked Potatoes alone.
3. On boiled Potatoes, given with grain or flour of grain.
4. On baked Potatoes, given with ſuch grain or flour.

The hogs to be as nearly alike in previous ſize and condition as may be; to be weighed when put to feeding in each caſe, as well as when killed. The quantity of each kind of feed to be particularized in each caſe; the calculation to be made at fair prices, and the plan of proceeding to be alike in both years. Not leſs than three hogs to each experiment; Five Guineas.

Claims to be made on or before the firſt of November 1791, and affidavits, if required, to be made of the accuracy of the accounts.

58. *Cart-Horſes.*—To the perſon who ſhall breed and rear for covering, within either of theſe four counties, the beſt Cart-Horſe; Five Guineas, or a Piece of Plate of equal value.

To be viewed by the Society's inſpectors at 3 years old.

Claims to be made prior to the annual meeting in 1793.

59. *Ram Lambs.*—To the perſon who, in proportion to the general ſize of his flock, ſhall breed and rear, from ſound ſtock, the largeſt quantity of the fineſt Ram Lambs, for the purpoſe of improving the breed of Sheep in theſe counties; Ten Guineas, or a Piece of Plate of equal value.

Notice to be given to the Secretary of an intention to claim the premium on or before Midſummer-Day 1790, that the lambs may be viewed prior to the firſt of November in the ſame year.

60. *Bulls for Stock.*—To the perſon who, reſiding in one of theſe four counties, who ſhall breed and rear the beſt Bull for the purpoſe of improving ſtock; Ten Guineas.

The bull to be viewed at two and three years old by the Society's inſpectors; and notice of an intention of claiming the premium to be given to the Secretary prior to Midſummer 1792.

61. *Rearing*

61. *Rearing Pigs.*—To the Farmer who ſhall breed and rear in the years 1790 and 1791 the greateſt quantity of Pigs, and keep the ſame till four months old, in either of the four counties; Five Guineas.

Satisfactory proofs of the number ſo raiſed to be produced to the Society on or before the November meeting in 1791.

62. *Natural Graſſes.*—To the perſon who, from actual experiments by ſeparate ſowings, on meaſured quantities of land, and by diſtinct feeding or cutting, ſhall ſatisfactorily aſcertain, and communicate in writing to this Society, the comparative value of the different Natural Graſſes now in uſe; the compariſon to lie both againſt each other, in feeding the different kinds of cattle, and againſt Artificial Graſſes, and green foddering crops, for the ſame purpoſe. The beſt method of culture to be pointed out, together with the ſoil beſt adapted to each ſpecies. Ten Guineas.

Timely notice to be given to the Secretary of an intention to claim for ſuch experiments, that the Society's Inſpectors may have opportunity of obſervation.

63. *Planting Timber-Trees.*—To the perſon who ſhall plant the largeſt tract of ground with Foreſt-Trees, for timber, ſuch as oak, elm, larch, firs, or poplar, not leſs than ten acres, nor leſs than one thouſand plants per acre; and who ſhall fence the ſame from cattle in a huſbandlike manner; Ten Guineas.

Notice to be given to the Secretary of an intention to claim this premium on or before Midſummer-Day next after the plantation ſhall have been finiſhed; and the ſame to be viewed by the Society's Inſpectors previous to the determination of the claim, at the November meeting the year following.

64. *Tranſplanting Rape.*—To the perſon who, in the year 1790, ſhall tranſplant from a ſeed-plot the greateſt quantity of Rape, not leſs than two acres, upon ridges from two to three feet aſunder, and from ſixteen to eighteen inches apart in the rows; and hand or horſe-hoe it in a workmanlike manner: And alſo with Rape ſow in the ſame field an equal quantity

quantity of land broad-caſt, and twice hand-hoe it, in order that it may be aſcertained which of the two is the beſt and moſt profitable method of cultivating that valuable plant as a food for cattle, ſheep, &c. Five Guineas, or a Piece of Plate of equal value.

Claims to be made on or before the firſt of Nov. 1790, previous to the feeding off the crops; which muſt, after ſuch claim, be fed off with the claimant's own ſtock. The whole expence of culture, with every particular reſpecting the profit ariſing from each diſtinct crop, and what ſort of ſtock was maintained upon them ſeparately, muſt be fully ſet forth to the Society on or before the 5th of July 1791.

To the perſon who in like manner ſhall tranſplant Rape, intended to ſtand for ſeed, and ſow in the ſame field an equal quantity of land, not leſs than one acre, and manage it as before directed, and ſhall deliver in a true account of the expence of cultivation, and the produce, and profit of each ſeparate crop; Five Guineas, or Plate of equal value.

Thoſe who intend to claim this Premium muſt give notice to the Secretary, previous to harveſting the Rape, that the crops may be viewed by the Society's Inſpectors.

65. *Planting Crab-Stocks in Hedges.*—To the perſon, whether landlord or tenant, who ſhall in the years 1790 or 1791, plant in the hedge-rows of his farm the greateſt quantity of Crab-Stocks; and who, when they are of proper age, ſhall graft them with Scions from ſome of the beſt ſorts of Cyder Fruits, and protect them from the bite of cattle, and report the ſucceſs and progreſs of the plantation to the Society, on or before the firſt of June 1796; Five Guineas, or Plate of equal value.

No claim to be admitted for a leſs quantity than four hundred, which muſt be deemed by the Society's Inſpectors thriving trees; nor muſt it be the deſign to tranſplant them afterwards into any orchard or other place, it being the wiſh of the Society to promote the increaſe of apple-trees, without injuring or incumbering paſture lands.

66. *Apple-Trees for Cyder.*—To the perſon who ſhall, in the years 1790 or 1791, plant upon his arable land the greateſt

greateſt quantity of Apple-Trees for Cyder Fruit, in direct lines, ſixty yards equidiſtant from each other, ſo as not to prevent the land from being eaſily ploughed, and ſhall fence and protect ſuch trees from the bite of cattle; Five Guineas, or Plate of equal value.

No claim to be admitted for a leſs number than four hundred trees; any claim for ſuch, or a larger number, to be made in or before the month of June 1793. Tall trees are recommended for this purpoſe, as being more out of the reach of cattle, and not ſo liable as dwarfs to injure the crop growing under them.

67. *Cyder of various Sorts.*—To the perſon who, from the growth of 1790 or 1791, ſhall make Cyder from the greateſt number of different ſorts of apples, keeping the ſorts perfectly unmixed. Thoſe ſorts to be not leſs than ſix, nor leſs than one hogſhead of Cyder to be made of each ſort. The Cyder to be made and managed as nearly alike as may be, put into perfectly ſound and ſweet caſks, and kept in the ſame cellar till Auguſt following; then to be taſted by appointment of the Society, and the ſorts accurately deſcribed; the Society to be at liberty to have a dozen bottles of each ſort, if they ſhall think proper, paying for the ſame. Ten Guineas. ——The ſeparate proceſs required, to be aſcertained to the Society's ſatisfaction.

N. B. The ſoundeſt keeping, and fineſt-flavoured fruits are recommended.

68. *Smut in Wheat.*—To the perſon who ſhall diſcover, and ſatisfactorily explain to this Society, the cauſe of Smut in Wheat, and point out an effectual remedy for the ſame, to be verified by experiments; Ten Guineas, or a recommendation to Parliament for a reward proportioned to the value of the diſcovery.

CLASS

CLASS II.

PREMIUMS for promoting MANUFACTURES.

1. *MALT-Making.*—To the perſon who ſhall clearly and fully aſcertain, from experiments on malting and brewing, the beſt proceſs of malt-making, ſo as from a given quantity of prime barley, of a given weight, to produce the greateſt quantity of beer, of a certain ſtrength, and of the fineſt flavour; Five Guineas.

2. *Marking Sheep.*—To the perſon who ſhall diſcover and make known to the Society any compoſition which ſhall be equally laſting with pitch and tar, for marking Sheep, without injuring the wool; Ten Guineas, or a Silver Cup of equal value.

A trial of one year, upon not leſs than twenty ſheep, and certificates of its fully anſwering the purpoſe, to be given in the firſt of July following the experiment.

3. *Writing Paper, and Package Paper.*—To the perſon who, in the years 1790 and 1791, ſhall make the greateſt quantity, not leſs than ten reams, or five bundles, of Writing, or other kinds of the moſt uſeful Package Paper, from vegetable ſubſtances not previouſly manufactured into thread, cloth, or cordage, and which ſhall be cheaper than ſimilar kinds of paper now in uſe; Ten Guineas, or a Piece of Plate of equal value.

Specimens of not leſs than one ream or bundle of each kind made, to be ſent to the Society at the meeting in September 1791, when claims are to be made with affidavits of the quantity, and that it is all of the claimant's own manufacture.

N. B. Specimens

N. B. Specimens of various papers made from potatoe-haulm, hop-binds, and other vegetable ſubſtances of Engliſh growth, may be ſeen at the London ſociety's room in the Adelphi.

4. *Madder.*—To the perſon who (not having cultivated this plant) ſhall, in autumn 1790, plant the largeſt quantity of land, not leſs than two acres, with Madder; and in the year 1794 ſhall produce the largeſt quantity of the root cured equally well, and which ſhall be as good for the purpoſe of dying, as that imported from Holland; Twenty Guineas.

A ſpecimen of not leſs than twenty pounds of the ſaid root to be produced at the Society's meeting in Nov. 1794, with certificates teſtifying that the reſt is of equal quality.

5. *Weld.*—To the perſon who, in the year 1790, ſhall produce the greateſt and beſt crop of Weld per acre, for the purpoſes of dying; Ten Guineas, or a Silver Cup of equal value. The quantity of land ſown to be not leſs than ſix acres.

N. B. This plant will thrive exceedingly well on the pooreſt ſoil.

For the two laſt Premiums there muſt be more than one claimant to each.

6. *Flax.*—To the perſon who, in the year 1790, ſhall raiſe, and properly break, dreſs, and prepare for market, the greateſt weight of Flax per acre, on the greateſt number of acres, not leſs than ten; Five Guineas.

Claims to be made, and the crop viewed before the Society's meeting in June 1790; and proper atteſtation made of the weight, before the February meeting 1791.

7. *Hemp.*—To the perſon who, in the year 1790, ſhall raiſe, and properly ſcale and prepare for market, the greateſt weight of Hemp per acre, on the greateſt number of acres, not leſs than eight; Five Guineas.

Claims to be made, and the crop viewed before the Society's meeting in June 1790; and proper atteſtation made of the weight, before the February meeting 1791.

CLASS

CLASS III.

PREMIUMS for IMPROVEMENTS in MECHANICS and ARTS.

1. *WOOL-Combing.*—To the person who shall contrive and describe a more simple, cheap, and healthy mode than any yet practised, of Combing Wool, by using common coal or other fuel instead of charcoal; or by introducing a Sand-Heat for the combs; simplicity and cheapness of the apparatus to be particularly attended to, and the success verified by satisfactory experiments; Five Guineas.

2. *Machine for Winding Wool.*—To the person who shall invent and describe a Machine for Spoling or Winding-off Worsted on Canes, and forming it into Warp at the same time, in the cheapest and most expeditious manner; Ten Guineas.

The merit of the invention to be verified by the testimony of woollen manufacturers from satisfactory experiments.

3. *Steam Corn-Mill.*—To the person who shall invent, and clearly describe, a cheap and useful Corn-Mill, to be worked by Steam, turning one pair of stones, grinding at least four Winchester bushels per hour, and dressing Meal at the same time as perfectly as a water-mill; Twenty Guineas.

The expence of the machinery and necessary building not to exceed 200l.

4. *Plough with two Horses or four Oxen.*—To the person who, in the year 1790, shall invent, or materially improve, any plough, so as to render it superior to any yet known, for the common uses of husbandry, and capable of being worked to advantage on strong clay land with two horses or four oxen; Five Guineas.

The

The merit of ſuch plough to be determined by the Committee of Farmers, from its performance at the publick trial of ploughs to be made in 1791.

5. *Drill-Plough.*—To the perſon who ſhall invent, and preſent to this Society, a Drill-Plough for general uſe, more ſimple and cheap in its conſtruction, and more perfect in its operation, than any general drill-plough yet known; Twelve Guineas.

6. *Cement for Ciſterns.*—To the perſon who ſhall invent a cheap and effectual compoſition, that ſhall completely anſwer the end of foreign Terras, in the cementing or lining of brick or ſtone ciſterns, ſo as to hold water as perfectly as lead will, either under or above ground; Five Guineas.

7. *Detection of unwholſome Ingredients in Beer.*—To the perſon who, from chemical analyſis, ſhall diſcover an eaſy and certain method of detecting the infuſion of any unwholſome Ingredient in ſmall or ſtrong Beer, ſold by common Brewers or Publicans; to the end that families may be enabled to detect ſuch dangerous impoſitions; Five Guineas.

8. *Machine for conveying Green Winter Crops off wet Arable Land.*—To the perſon who ſhall invent and conſtruct the ſimpleſt and moſt uſeful Machine for conveying Green Winter Crops off wet Arable Land, by means of which the work may be done cheaper, and with leſs poaching, or other injury to the land than by any method now practiſed; Ten Guineas, or a Silver Cup of that value.

The machine, or a complete model of it, to be produced to the Society at or before the meeting in September 1790 or 1791; and proper time for trial allowed.

9. *Deſtroying Vapours in Coal-Mines.*—To the perſon who ſhall conſtruct a portable apparatus, on a better and more eligible plan than thoſe now in uſe at Newcaſtle, or elſewhere, and which ſhall be capable of effectually deſtroying or expelling the noxious Vapours in Coal-Mines; Ten Guineas.

If the ſaid apparatus or machine will not only fully anſwer the above purpoſe, but alſo produce ſufficient light for working Coal-Mines, without burning candles or lamps in them, this Premium will be enlarged to Twenty Guineas.

A model or models of the ſaid apparatus to be produced, and claims made on or before the firſt of January 1791.

10. *Deſtroying Smoke in Glaſs-Houſes.*—To the perſon who ſhall diſcover and make known to the Society, on or before the firſt of October 1791, a cheap, eaſy, and effectual method of deſtroying the Smoke of Glaſs-Houſes, Fire-Engines, Furnaces, &c. aſcertained by experiments properly atteſted, in order to prevent their being an annoyance to the neighbourhood; an Honorary Premium of Plate.

11. *Plough for Potatoe Crops.*—Three Guineas or a Piece of Plate of equal value, will be given to the inventor of the beſt new-conſtructed Plough for ploughing up Potatoe Crops, by which the work may be done with the leaſt loſs or damage to the crop. The ſaid plough to be ſent to the Society on or before the firſt of September 1790, that trials may be made previous to the meeting in November.

12. *Machine for Floating Paſture Lands.*—To the perſon who ſhall invent and make a better Machine than has yet been conſtructed, for raiſing Water to float Paſture Lands; Twenty Guineas.

The ſaid Machine to be worked either by wind or water, and to raiſe water at leaſt four feet above the ſurface of the ſtream whereon it is placed.

A model of the ſaid Machine, with a certificate teſtifying that the Machine itſelf has been worked, and found effectually to anſwer the purpoſe, to be produced at or before the Society's meeting in November 1790.

N. B. The more ſimple and cheap the conſtruction, and the leſs attendance required, the greater will be its merit.

13. *Hand-Mill.*—To the perſon who ſhall conſtruct and preſent to the Society, on or before the firſt of September 1790, the beſt Hand-mill for grinding wheat for private families, which ſhall be different from, and for ſimplicity, cheapneſs, and effect ſuperior to any now in uſe; Ten Guineas, or a Silver Cup of that Value.

14. *Italian Method of Killing Cattle.*—A Silver Cup of Five Guineas value will be given to the Butcher, who, in the year 1790, ſhall kill the greateſt number of Horned Cattle,

Sheep

Sheep, and Hogs, in the method, and with the ſame kind of inſtrument uſed for that purpoſe at Naples, and recommended by Sir *William Hamilton* in his letter to the Society.

The number of Horned Cattle ſo killed to be not leſs than 20, and of Hogs and Sheep not leſs than 50 each.

Claims, and certificates on oath, to be produced on or before the firſt of September 1791.

A correct drawing of this inſtrument may be ſeen at the Society's Room, with directions how to uſe it.

15. *Securing Buildings from Fire.*—For the beſt method of effectually preventing accidental Fires in Houſes or other Buildings, by a cheaper method than has been hitherto ſuggeſted; Ten Guineas, or a Piece of Plate of equal value.

16. *Greateſt Stock of Bees.*—To the perſon who, in the year 1790, ſhall raiſe, under his own care and inſpection, the greateſt number of Stocks of Bees, not leſs than twenty; Three Guineas, or a Piece of Plate of equal value.

17. *Honey or Wax without deſtroying the Bees.*—To the perſon who, in the year 1790, ſhall produce the greateſt quantity of Honey or Wax, from Bees of his own raiſing, and that without deſtroying the Bees; Three Guineas, or a Piece of Plate of equal value.

N. B. Claims for the laſt two Premiums to be made before the firſt of November 1790.

18. *Friendly Societies.*—A Premium of Ten Guineas will be given to the moſt numerous Friendly Society, conſiſting chiefly of Handicraftsmen and Labourers, which ſhall, before the firſt day of January 1791, be eſtabliſhed in any town or pariſh, within either of the four counties, where no ſuch Society now ſubſiſts.

The Conditions of this Premium are,

1ſt. That the Society ſhall have been eſtabliſhed one year, and conſiſt of not fewer than forty Members when the claim is made.

2dly. That none of the ſaid members ſhall have belonged to any other club of this kind ſince the firſt of Jan. 1789.

3dly. That no Society ſhall be entitled to this premium, unleſs there be a clauſe inſerted in their Articles, that no part of their ſtock ſhall ever be laid out in the purchaſe of

Lottery Tickets, or in any other way which may risque any part of their property in games of chance.

4thly. That as soon as their fund amounts to 100l. one half of it shall be laid out in government or land security.

5thly. That should it increase in future so as to enable them to make any division of their principal among the members, they shall always on making such division leave at least one hundred pounds in stock.

6thly. That every Society intending to claim this premium shall, at the time of its institution, send a fair copy of their Articles to this Society for inspection before printing them.

7thly. That each claim shall be accompanied with a certificate, signed by the Minister and Churchwardens of the parish; containing a printed copy of their Articles, the amount of their stock, and the number of actual members, with their names and occupations.

Claims to be made at the meeting in September 1791.

It is recommended to Farmers, &c. to promote these Societies, by becoming members of them, as they evidently tend to lessen the Poor's Rates.

PLOUGHING.—As in the whole circle of Agricultural practice, there is nothing more interesting to the Farmer than *Ploughing well* and *cheap*; the following Premiums are offered, that a fair and general comparative trial may take place in March or April next, of the various Ploughs of different constructions:

For the Plough that performs best, Six Guineas.

For the second-best, Four Guineas.

For the third-best, if it has any real merit, Two Guineas.

And that rewards be also given to the Ploughmen, viz.

To the Ploughman of the first-best, a Pair of Buck-skin Breeches, or a Guinea.

To the second-best, a Pair of strong Sheep-skin ditto, or Half-a-Guinea.

To the third-best, a Smock Frock, or a Crown.

Particulars of the day and place to be agreed on at the February meeting, and advertised in their resolutions.

The following Forms of Certificates on Behalf of Servants and Labourers claiming the Bounty of this Society, are required to be obſerved, viz.

No. I.

CERTIFICATE *of a* SERVANT'S GOOD BEHAVIOUR.

Pariſh of , *in the county of* , *Oct.* , 1790.

THIS certifies that has lived with as a yearly ſervant, wholly employed in huſbandry, during years, ending the of laſt; that was not a pariſh apprentice; and that conduct during the whole time has been honeſt, ſober, orderly, and induſtrious: as ſuch beg leave to recommend as worthy the reward of the Bath Agriculture Society.

——— ——— Maſter
——— ——— Miſtreſs.

WE whoſe names are hereunto ſubſcribed, do declare that the above-written parties are well known to us, and that we believe the account to be ſtrictly true.

——— ——— } Miniſter of ——— aforeſaid.

——— ——— } Churchwardens
——— ——— } *or* Overſeers.

To the Society for the Encouragement of Agriculture, &c. at Bath.

No. II.

No. II.

CERTIFICATE *of* INDUSTRY *and bringing up a* FAMILY.

Pariſh of , *in the county of* , *Oct.* , 1790.

THIS certifies that , a labourer in huſbandry, of the pariſh of in the county of , to the beſt of our knowledge and belief, and according to his own declaration made to us, has had born to him legitimate children, of whom he has maintained and brought up (the youngeſt being more than 7 years of age) by his own labour in huſbandry only, without receiving any parochial aſſiſtance; and not having rented during any part of the aforeſaid period more than 4l. per annum.

——— ——— Preſent Maſter.

——— ——— } Miniſter of the pariſh aforeſaid

——— ——— } Churchwardens
——— ——— } *or* Overſeers.

To the Society for the Encouragement of Agriculture, &c. at Bath.

No. III.

Form of a NOTICE *to be given by Servants, intending to claim for faithful Servitude, according to the Rule in ſuch Caſes.*

Pariſh of , *in the county of* , *Oct.* , 1790.

SIR,

I beg you to inform the Nobility and Gentlemen of the Bath Agriculture Society, that having lived a hired yearly ſervant in the ſtation of with of this pariſh, during years, ending the of laſt; I intend, if it pleaſe divine Providence to grant me life and ability, ſo to live in ſobriety, induſtry, and fidelity, in the ſame place, as at the end of five years from the expiration of my laſt, to claim a Premium of the Bath Society, with ſucceſs.

Witneſs my hand,

—— ——.

To the Secretary of the Bath Agriculture Society.

N. B. All certificates reſpecting Servitude and Induſtry to be ſent in before the firſt of November in each year.

☞ An

An improved MACHINE for Winnowing and Cleaning various kinds of GRAIN and SEEDS, has lately been approved by this Society. It is recommended as valuable for its complete and expeditious performance, and may be ſeen at the Society's Rooms. Price Nine Guineas.

N. B. Seeds, and Seed-Corn, of the beſt quality, and adapted for change on different ſoils, may be had, at reaſonable rates, by application to the Secretary; who alſo ſuperintends the Conſtruction of any Implements of Huſbandry, (not being patent) which are particularly approved by the Society, and ſends them according to order to any part of the Kingdom.

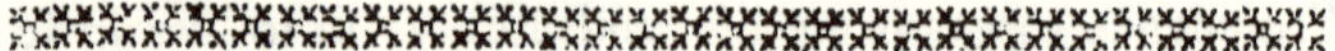

GENERAL CONDITIONS.

Although in wording the foregoing Premiums, care has been taken to guard againſt improper Claims, the Society think it expedient to add, that their deſign is not to reward thoſe who are already Good Farmers for what happens to be their uſual mode of practice; but to increaſe the number of ſuch, by exciting a ſpirit of emulation in others to follow their example; and to indemnify them for any extra expence or loſs they may ſuſtain from new experiments. And therefore, to prevent any claimant from gaining any Premium, who, although he may have complied in his uſual courſe of practice with the mere letter of the premium offered, has done nothing new to obtain it, the following GENERAL CONDITIONS *are added.*

THE Society reſerve to themſelves the power of giving, in ſuch caſes, ſuch part only of any premium as the performance ſhall be judged to deſerve; or of withholding the whole, if there be no merit.

To prevent partiality, it is required, that all matters for which premiums are claimed, be delivered in without names, or any intimation to whom

whom they belong. That each particular model, ſpecimen, deſign, &c. be marked in what manner the claimants ſhall think fit, each claimant ſending with it a ſealed paper, having on the outſide a correſponding mark, and on the inſide his name and addreſs.

No papers ſhall be opened but ſuch as ſhall gain Premiums, unleſs where it appears abſolutely neceſſary for the determination of the claim. All the reſt ſhall be returned unopened, with the marks to which they belong, if enquired after by their marks within two years. If not demanded, they ſhall be publickly burnt, unopened, at ſome meeting of the Society.

The claims ſhall be determined at the Annual meeting next after which they are made, except in caſes where the premium is extended to another year.

A

L I S T

OF THE

PREMIUMS and BOUNTIES

GIVEN BY THIS SOCIETY.

	£.	s.	d.
TO 27 Claimants in Agriculture ——	169	14	0
To 9 ditto in Mechanicks — —	47	5	6
To 3 ditto in Gardening and Botany ——	26	5	0
To 1 ditto for improving Cattle — —	5	5	0
To 5 ditto in Manufactures — ——	19	19	0
To 2 ditto, Women reaping — —	4	4	0
To 3 ditto, Essays on Agriculture ——	34	13	0
To 2 ditto, Friendly Societies — —	21	0	0
To 3 ditto for Prizes at public trial of Ploughs	14	14	0
To 13 ditto, Labourers in Husbandry, for bringing up large families without parochial aid	37	16	0
To 82 Servants in Husbandry for long and faithful Servitude —— —— ——	214	4	0
Amount of Premiums prior to the year 1789	£.594	19	6

Premiums given for the Year 1789.

SOMERSETSHIRE.

	£.	s.	d.
To Mr. James Smith of Corston, for rearing a Dozen excellent Ram-lambs, for improving the breed of Sheep —— ——	10	10	0
To Mr. Thomas Parsons, for the raising and management of a fine crop of Flax ——	5	5	0

To

	£.	s.	d.
Brought forward	15	15	0
To Mr. Lawrence Fielde, for Plans and Elevations of Cottages for Gentlemen's Eſtates	3	3	0
To Richard Hatch, for burning 140 buſhels of Fern-Aſhes — — —	3	3	0
To Mr H. Murrell, for the invention of a valuable Waſhing Machine — —	3	3	0
To James Sutton, for 27 years Servitude —	2	2	0
To Mary Hawkins, for 44 years ditto —	2	2	0
To Joſeph Hewlett, for bringing up 11 children without parochial aid — —	3	3	0

WILTSHIRE.

	£.	s.	d.
To Thomas Crook, eſq; for rearing a number of Calves without milk — —	6	6	0
To William Herne, for 60 years Servitude —	2	2	0
To William Harris, labourer in huſbandry, for bringing up 7 children without parochial aid	3	3	0
To Henry Hill, labourer in huſbandry, for bringing up 6 children in the ſame manner —	2	2	0

GLOCESTERSHIRE.

	£.	s.	d.
To Mr. Lewin Tugwell, for raiſing and twice hand-hoing a large crop of Turnips —	7	7	0
To Sarah Bryant, for 27 years Servitude —	2	2	0
To William Palmer, labourer in huſbandry, for bringing up 10 children without parochial aid	3	3	0
To William Brewer, labourer in huſbandry, for bringing up 8 children in the ſame manner	2	2	0
To Ann Lawrence, for reaping 13 acres of Wheat	3	3	0

DORSETSHIRE.

	£.	s.	d.
To James Arnell, for 37 years Servitude —	2	2	0
To Roſe Buſh, for 38 years ditto —	2	2	0
Total of Premiums given, for the year 1789	68	5	0
Total of ditto for the preceding years	594	19	6
Total of Premiums given by this Society	£. 663	4	6

NAMES

NAMES of the preſent MEMBERS

ALPHABETICALLY ARRANGED.

Their Graces the Dukes of BUCCLEUGH, MARLBOROUGH, and NEWCASTLE.

MARQUISES of GRAHAM, and LADSDOWN.

The EARLS of

AILESBURY
CORK
COURTOWN
DARTMOUTH
ILCHESTER
SHAFTESBURY
AND
WINCHELSEA.

LORDS

AUDLEY
BATEMAN
BAYHAM
BULKLEY
DIGBY
DE MONTALT
PETRE
RIVERS
AND
SHERBORNE.

BARON DIMSDALE.

His Highneſs the PRINCE of DASHCAW.

COUNT RICE.—COUNT SALIS.

A.

ANDERDON R. P. eſq; Henlade, near Taunton
Acland Sir Tho. Dyke, bart.
Acland Hugh, eſq; Bath
Ames Levi, eſq; Charlton
Atwood Rich. eſq; Turley
Anderdon Wm. eſq; Bath
Anſtie John, eſq; Devizes
Alexander Mr. Maningford
Albyn Rev. Mr. Saint
Aldworth Rich. eſq; Ireland
Anningſon Luck, eſq; Bath
Audry John, eſq; Seend
Aſtley F. D. eſq; Everley
Ames Levi, eſq; Briſtol

B.

Blagrave John, eſq;
Barclay Robert, eſq; London
Baſkerville Major

Barnewall

Barnewall Michael, esq;
Barter Rev. Wm. Brudenell, Timsbury
Broughton Rev. J. Twerton
Barnes Mr. George, Mells
Brydges Francis W. T. esq; Tibberton, Herefordshire
Bush Robert, esq; Tracy-Park
Butler John, esq; Martock
Bovet Rich. esq; Wellington
Bright Lowbridge, esq; Bristol
Bright William, esq; Bristol
Bolton ——, esq; Ireland
Bathurst Pool, esq; Alton, Dorsetshire
Barwis Wm. M. D. Devizes
Brickdale Matthew, esq; M.P. Monckton
Barnard James, esq; Crowcombe
Ballard Wm. Aldridge, esq; Bratton, Wilts
Barry Redmond, esq; Bath
Billingsley John, esq; Ashwick-Grove
Beaufoy H. esq; London
Bethel Mr. G. Bradford
Boswell Mr. G. Piddletown
Baylis Mr. Robt. Westerleigh
Bartley Mr. Nehemiah, Bristol
Bradley Mr. Mells
Burgh Henry, esq; Stroud
Bretton Mr. Lionel, Bath
Bonnor Mr. engraver

C.

Corbett Sir Corbett, bart. Adderly Hall, Salop
Cam Samuel, esq; Bradford
Cotton Thomas, esq; near Barnsley
Coxe C. Westley, esq; Bath
Cox Laurence, esq; near Dorchester
Cox Joseph Mason, M. D. Fish-Ponds
Curtis John Adey, esq; Oxford
Colborne Benj. esq; Bath
Chapman Anth. esq; Woolcombe-Hall, Dorset
Coxe Henry Hippesley, esq; Ston-Easton
Coxe Charles, esq.
Crook Mr. T. Tytherington
Collins J. esq; Hatch-court
Cleobury Rev. Dr. Bath
Clark Richard Hall, esq; near Honiton
Collins Mr. B. C. Salisbury
Coke T. W. esq; Holkham-Hall, Norfolk
Clavill William, esq; Bath
Cruttwell Mr. W. Sherborne
Cruttwell Mr. Richard, Bath
Creswell Estcourt, esq; Bibery
Cross Rich. esq; Broomfield
Crossley Wm. esq; Bath
Collett Mr. Isaac, Bath
Cole John, esq; Arnolds, near Dorking, Surry
Clark Mr. Wm. Bath
Claridge M. esq; London
Clutterbuck Rev. Lewis, Ozleworth, Glocestershire

D.

Duntze Sir John, Rockbere, Devon
Durbin Sir John, Bristol
Damer Hon. Lionel
Daniel Samuel, esq; Yeovil
Dickinson Barnard, esq; Monks
Drax Tho. Earle, esq; Charborough-hall, Dorset
Derham Mr. Henry, Bath
Darch Major, Hill-Bishops
Dumaresq Rev. Dr. Yeovilton
Davis Tho. esq; Long-Leat
Dawson Benj. esq; Bath
Dyke Wm. esq; Syrencot
Dyke Mr. Daniel, Sarum

Estcourt

E.

Eſtcourt T. eſq; Gloceſterſh.
Earl W. Benſon, eſq; Sarum
Evill Mr. William, Bath
Everit J. Gale, eſq; Heyteſbury
Everit Wm. eſq; ditto

F.

Falconer William, M. D. F. R. S. Bath
Fothergill Anthony, M. D. F. R. S. Bath
Frazer Wm. M. D. Bath
Forteſcue R. Inglet, eſq; Devon
Freke Rev. J. Wyke, Dorſet
Foſter Mr. John, Bath
Fitchew Mr. Cha. Devizes
Fox Mr. Tho. Wellington
Franklin J. eſq; near Cowbridge, South-Wales
Freeman Tho. Edward, jun. eſq; Gloceſterſhire
Fielde Mr. Laurence, Bath

G.

Grenville Hon. James, M.P. Butleigh
Guiſe Sir John, bart.
Gordon Mr. James, London
Goldney S. eſq; Bath
Gibbs Gaisford, eſq; Weſtbury
Greenaway Giles, eſq; Burrington
Gale Mr. John, Stert
Gent Mr. James, Devizes
Gabriel Rev. Dr. Bath
Goadby Mr. Sherborne
Garnet John, eſq; Briſtol
Gurney Bartlett, eſq; Norwich
Goldwire Mr. Briſtol
Greathead Ed. eſq; Uddens, near Wimborne, Dorſet
Gordon John, jun. eſq; Briſtol
Gould Rev. Mr. Luckham

H.

Hawkins Chriſt. eſq; Trewithen, Cornwall, M. P.
Hawkins Mr. Down-Emney
Hoare Sir Richard Colt, bart.
Harington Edward, eſq; Bath
Harington Rev. Dr. Thruxton
Hamilton Charles, eſq.
Hellier Mr. Stourton
Hinton Mr. J. Horningſham
Harris Mr. Cha. London
Harvey Dr. Briſlington
Hoare Edward, eſq;
Horner Tho. eſq; Mells-Park
Hackett Andrew, eſq; Muxhall, Warwickſhire
Horlock Iſaac Webb, eſq;
Hazard Mr. Joſiah, Holt
Harford Joſeph, eſq; Briſtol
Harford Ch. Joſ. eſq; Briſtol
Harris Thomas, eſq; Briſtol
Hinton Wm. eſq; Biſhopſtrow
Hawker Wm. eſq; Pitminſter
Hyatt Mr. T. Shepton
Hazard Mr. Samuel, Bath
Harriſon Mr. near Marſhfield
Hewit Mr. J. Rolſton
Hooper Mr. John, Bath
Hellicar Mr. jun. Briſtol
Head J. Roper, eſq; Wookey
Higgs Mr. Thomas, Sodbury

J.

Jones Sir William Langham, Ramſbury Manor, Wilts
Jacks Mr. Walter, Briſtol
James W. S. eſq;
Jekyl Joſeph, eſq; Spetiſbury
Jones John, eſq; jun. Bradford

K.

Kent Rev. Dr. Pottern
Kirkpatrick Joſeph, eſq;

King

King James, esq; M. C. Lower-Rooms, Bath
Knatchbull Capt.
Keppell ——, esq; Presbury

L.

Long Sir James Tylney, bart. M. P.
Lettsom J. Coakley, M. D. F. R. S. S. A. London
Locke Thomas, esq; Devizes
Ludlow Mr. Daniel, Sodbury
Lediard Mr. John, Melksham
Lysons Daniel, M. D. Bath
Lovell Rev. Archdea. Wells
Lethbridge John, esq;
Lowder John, esq; Bath Bank
Lovell John, esq; Wells
Luttrell Rev. A. F. St. Audries

M.

Miller Sir John Riggs, bart. M. P. Bath-Easton
Molesworth Sir Wm. bart.
Master Thomas, esq; M. P.
Moysey Abel, esq; Member for Bath
Mandel Mr. William, Bath
Matravers Mr. Wellington
Meares Robert, esq; Frome
Messiter R. esq; Wincanton
Murrell Mr. Henry, Bath

N.

Nash Sir Stephen, Bristol
Nagle Joseph, esq; Bath
Nihel Dr. Circus, Bath
Noad Mr. Jonathan, Road
Neate Thomas, esq; Bath
Newman Mr. John, Norton St. Phillips

O.

Orchard Paul, esq; Hartland Abbey
Orchard Mr. Walter, Bath

P.

Palk Sir Robert, bart. M. P.
Paul Sir G. O. bart.
Phelips Edw. esq; Montacute
Phelips Edw. esq; Member for Somersetshire
Pickwick Mr. Eleazer, Bath
Patten Thomas, esq; Bath
Phillott Charles, esq; Bath
Provis Wm. esq; Shepton
Palmer John, esq; London
Parry Caleb H. M. D. Bath
Parsons Mr. Tho. Blagden
Pine Mr. William, Bristol
Pike Mr. near Devizes
Piercy J. Stoke near Lavington
Perrot George, esq; Pershore, Worcestershire
Perry Mr. John, Bath
Peacey Mr. Wm. Northleach
Pugh B. esq; Midford Castle

R.

Robertson M. S. M. D. Bath
Rogers John, esq; Yarlington
Rolle Dennis, esq; Shapwick
Rogers Rev. J. Berkeley
Reynolds Mr. Rich. Ketley
Reynolds Edm. esq; Milford, near Lymington, Hants
Robins Mr. Thomas, Bristol
Richardson Mr. Rich. Devizes
Rudhall Mr. printer, Bristol
Randal Mr. Matth. Devizes
Rich Julius Samuel, esq; Trowbridge
Randolph Rev. Mr. Corston
Rashleigh P. esq; M. P. Manabilly, near Fowey

S.

Smith Sir John, bart. Sydling St. Nicholas, Dorset
Scudamore Lieut. Col. M. P. near Hereford

Stephens Jas. esq; Camerton
Sutton James, esq; Devizes
Stephens Sam. esq; Tregony Castle
Strachey Henry, esq; M. P. Sutton-Court
Sainsbury William, esq; Bath
Smith Robert, esq; M. P. for Nottingham
Savery John, esq; Butcombe-House
Sanford H. W. esq; Monckton
Sandford Rev. Mr. Sandford-Hall
Smith Rev. M. S. Prior-Park
Sibley Rev. J. Walcot
Swaine Rev. G. Pucklechurch
Shirley Edward, esq; Wood-End, Glocestershire
Shirley Evelyn, esq;
Sheppard Mr. Walter, Frome
Sandford ——, esq; Bath
Sanders Mr. Tho. Bristol
Smith J. esq; Devizes, M. P.
Smith Ralph, esq; Gay Brook, Ireland
Shafto Robert, esq; Barford, Wilts
Smith John, esq; Combhay
Smith Mr. James, Corston
Smith Samuel, esq; London
Smith Benj. esq; London
Selden Mr. Wm. Bath
Smith Capt. Wm. Sidney
Sweet Rev. Tho. Baliol College, Oxon

T.

Trevelyan Sir John, bart. Member for Somersetshire
Trenchard William, esq;
Turner N. esq; Ipswich
Tylee Mr. John, Devizes
Trelawney Rev. Sir Harry
Tooker James, esq;
Tugwell Mr. Lewen
Tanner D. esq; Monmouth

V.

Vaughan Mr. Geo. Preston
Vagg Mr. Hen. Chilcompton
Vernon Rev. Edw. Bourton on the Water
Vivian Rev. Mr. Withiel, Cornwall

W.

Winnington Sir Edward, bart. Winterdyne, Worcestersh.
Wrey Sir Bouchier, bart. Tawstock, Devon
Watson Wm. esq; F. R. S. Bath
Waller Edm. esq; Farmington
Whitehead John, esq; London
Wolffe C. G. esq; London
Wadman John, esq; Imberhall
Williams J. H. esq; Wales
Walcot Edmund, esq;
Williams P. esq; near Brecon
Wentworth Fred. Tho. esq; Henbury
Willis Rev. Thomas, Bath
Were Mr. Nich. Wellington
White John, esq; Ilchester
Wright Nathan, esq; Bath
Woolcombe Dr. Bath
Winter Mr. Geo. Bristol
Whitaker William, esq;
Webb John, gent. Doynton
Webb Mr. Francis
Winter Tho. Bradbury, esq; Frome
Whitmarsh John, esq; Taunton.

Honorary and Correſpondent Members.

Monſ. Poitevin, Preſident of the Royal Society of Montpellier.

Monſ. Roland de la Platiere, Inſpector-General of the Manufactures in France.

Monſ. De Rully, Count of Lyons, Preſident of the Royal Society there.

Monſ. l'Abbé de Vitré, Secretary of the aforeſaid Society.

Monſ. Froſſard, L. L. D. Miniſter of the Proteſtant Church at Lyons.

Hon. Mr. Charles de Heithauſen, Sileſia.

Adam James, eſq; London
Anderſon Dr. Jas. Scotland
Beevor Sir Thomas, bart. Hethel-Hall, Norfolk
Blunt Sir Charles, Croydon
Bernard Tho. eſq; Romſey
Beeſly Mr. James, London
Barclay David, eſq; Herts
Bakewell Mr. Diſhley
Clendon Rev. Mr. King's-Brumpton
Cooke Rev. Mr. London
Cloſe Rev. H. J. Ipſwich, Suffolk
Dobſon Mr. Norwich
Fordyce Dr. Geo. London
Grieve Dr. John, F.R.A. SS. Edinburgh, and late Phyſician to the Ruſſian army
Gullet Chriſt. eſq; Exeter
Grimwood Mr. Kenſington
Hunter Dr. York
Hinton Dr. Norfolk
Hill Chriſt. eſq; Darlington
Hawes Rev. Mr. Box
Howman Rev. Mr. Norfolk
Howell Rev. Mr. Poole
Hill Rev. Mr. Kent
Ingenhouz Dr. Vienna
Ireland Rev. Dr.
Kett Mr. Tho. Norwich
Komove Monſ. from Peterſburgh
Kirby J. eſq; Ipſwich
Marſhall Mr. Norfolk
Moreau Simeon, eſq; M. C. Cheltenham
More Samuel, eſq; London
Manſel Sir William, near Carmarthen
Portarlington Right Hon. Earl of
Prieſtley Joſ. LL.D. F.R.S.
Pollet Mr. Bardfield, Eſſex
Pryce Mr. Benj. Saliſbury
Phillips Mr. Rich. Redruth
Sanſom Philip, eſq; London
Sheffield Lord
Staples Sir Robert, bart.
Sanders Rev. Mr. Sidmouth
Turner Rev. David, Secretary to the Cardigan Society
Woods Mr. Joſeph, London
Wagſtaff Mr. John, Norwich
Wimpey Mr. Joſeph
Woodbine Wm. eſq; Norfolk
Yeldham J. jun. eſq; F.A.S.
Young Arthur, eſq.

www.ingramcontent.com/pod-product-compliance
Lightning Source LLC
Chambersburg PA
CBHW021628270326
41931CB00008B/919